# When You Walked Away

# When You Walked Away

Iris Bailey

# Table of Contents

**Part 1:**



**Part 2:**



**Part 3:**

*For those that have been*

*left in the dark*

# 1. Lost

They say it takes you loving yourself

Before you can love another person.
I don't believe that's true.
I think you can love another,
So much more than yourself that it becomes toxic.

Since we don't always know what we deserve,
We end up giving all the love we have
To someone else unreturned.
Silently, we wonder
Where the love we're supposed to feel had gone?

So we <u>should</u> love ourselves before loving someone else,
Unfortunately sometimes we just <u>can't</u>.

Love is one of the most intricate things I have ever experienced.
It's so extremely fulfilling yet can leave you absolutely empty.
You're either everything or nothing.

No inbetween.
Not one or the other.
<u>But sometimes even both.</u>

It's a funny word, love.
You see some people believe
That's all it is.
And that's all it'll ever be.
It's a word that might've meant something,
But due to our corrupted minds,
Now simply means nothing.

<u>I love you.</u>
But you're walking away?

<u>I still love you.</u>
But you left?

<u>I will always love you.</u>
Then why didn't you stay?

We believe love is fake.
And that people don't mean it,
When they desperately form that word
In a sentence.

Unfortunately, we say this to ourselves,
In hopes of believing it's just a hoax,
And sparing our hearts from the hurt
We all know and are so used to.

Truth is,
Love is all around us.
Just because we don't think we experience it,
Does not mean we haven't.

It's just easier to accept it doesn't exist all together,
Than to accept the one we thought
We might share it with,
<u>Wasn't</u>
<u>Meant</u>
<u>To be.</u>

On the other hand,
We are so desperate to feel it,
That we settle for things,
And call it <u>love.</u>

Confusing our minds
And damaging our hearts
Has been such a common result.
Going about the world,
Like a pandemic.

It's a funny word,
That does funny things.
But it behaves differently for everyone.
So, we can't prepare ourselves for it,
And we most definitely can't study it,

Therefore, we describe it using one word
that doesn't ever seem to be enough-

Love.

Screaming it over and over again,
Seeking to convince myself that it's true.
I repeat
<u>It's different.</u>
<u>It isn't like that with us.</u>

I always thought love involved two people.
Like Christmas, where you give and receive.
I later understood the popularity of unrequited love in today's society.
Unfortunately, without knowing, I decided to give it a try myself.

Realizing I was the only one feeling a certain way,
In whatever confusing relationship I previously had,
My whole view of it changed.

I stopped seeing things in rose colored glasses.
Took off the enhanced saturation.
And finally saw how dark and dull the world around us could be.

Without any light to guide me,
It was easy to wander.

Eventually, I strayed too far,
And lost myself in the dark.

My insecurities took complete control
Of my behavior,
The way I think,
And how I react.
Everything around me suddenly became so much worse.

It felt like I had fallen from the sky,
Into the deep blue ocean,
Being washed away, drifting back and forth.

<u>I was going through the motions.</u>
My body there but my mind elsewhere.

And you would think when I can't breathe
I'd come up for air.
Instead, I lay there drowning.
Without reaching out for help.

I'm too afraid if I call,
No one will be there to answer.
So I'm sinking,
With my insides inescapably flooding.

Is their abandonment my fault?
I used to believe there was <u>someone</u> for everyone,
That we're all destined for a partner.
But I guess some of us are just destined to be alone,
Wondering where we went wrong.

I just didn't feel wanted anymore.

How could I help myself,
When I was acting as the main source of most of my problems.
I'm standing in my own way,
Not letting anyone get to me because my body is so full of fear.

Logically, I was never really good at making decisions.
My heart would always be the one in charge.

It's also why it frequently got hurt.
I was my own worst enemy.

I thought I was saving myself the pain,
Refusing to make difficult decisions.

<u>Just dealing</u>
<u>Managing</u>
<u>Waiting for it to get better.</u>

The longer it went on,
The more I realized it was a pattern I had to break.

I had to do this for myself.
I had to do this because
I knew I would be the only one who would.

Attempting to cope, I developed unnecessary methods.
Becoming obsessed with the red lines
I'd paint all over my skin.
They'd dry out and I'd do it again.
<u>Over and over, like an unbreakable habit.</u>

Ironically,
It became a cycle when the reason for self harm,
Would simply be because of it.

Disappointed-
In myself-
Due to others-

<u>That's all I've ever felt.</u>

Over time the scars have faded.
But not completely disappearing,
Just like I'd hoped when creating them.
To remind myself what I am:

Broken
Damaged
And an unlovable charity case

It was addicting.
Too addicting.
Sadly, the world is far from pretty,
And if I ever said I haven't been way too close
To not living in it,
<u>I would be lying.</u>

Growing up
Came a bit sooner than expected,
And I was constantly reminded in my dreams.

This little girl would go up to her broken self,
In her clear, polished, mirror.
Looking back at her own image,
Mumbling through her own sobs,

<u>You deserve this</u>

Except I was wide awake.
Not dreams, but memories.
Memories I cannot forget.
Because even if I try,
<u>The faded lines are there to remind me.</u>

I was only so young and felt the weight of the world.
Crushing me down little by little.

I can't get up anymore.
I'm falling through the surface,
Like I'm almost melting.

Funny how I wasn't ever
Strong enough to be solid.

But you found me.

You found me and my body deteriorated with chemicals.
Seeing how visibly broken I was,
you saved me anyway.

You were there when the reek of alcohol invaded my room,
And the empty pill bottles decorated my furniture.

In my time of need,
<u>You were there</u>
<u>You are here</u>
<u>And you will always be everywhere.</u>

# 2. Found

I don't believe in love at first sight,
But I swear, the moment I met you,
I knew you would take up the space in my heart...
I just didn't know you'd also be what left a hole in it.

You told me you loved me,
Yet proved the opposite,
Every time you opened your mouth.

Like a pool of liquid,
Honesty pours out of you,
Flooding the ground.

The worst part is I might've believed you and your love,
If you weren't so visibly filled with hatred and neglect.

It would've been so easy between us,
If you just let it.

But instead,
Your fear took over,
And the self sabotaging began.

<u>They say if you love someone, let them go...</u>

But why?

Why must I always let you go

When I've worked so hard to have you?

Why do our expectations fall upon

Something that isn't even physically possible?

Nothing is permanent.

So let me have you whilst I still can...

Now I lie awake in bed,
Tracing the parts of my body that you once touched.
Knowing I'll miss that forever.
And knowing I'll never not remember.

I still recall
Every one of
Your features vividly.
Like I'd only just seen you.

You were so beautiful.
I could stare at your deep brown, chestnut eyes,
Forever, reminiscing in the past.

The nostalgia overriding my body,
Makes me remember who we once were.
And who we will never be again.

I still remember the way my fingers would
Comb through your curly, fluffy, just as brown, hair.
I remember when you decided to change your haircut,
Showing more angles of your face I haven't seen,
Loving every single inch of you day after day.

I remember when you grew the stubble on your chin.
And right after you shaved,
I could feel the warm embrace of your skin.
Yours touching mine.
It felt like the safest place for me to be.

I loved every single thing about you.
<u>I still do.</u>
<u>You are still my home.</u>

Growing up, I was always a cheesy romantic.
I fail to say I'm not anymore.

I always think back to the memory of us first dancing.
In your bedroom, with candles lit,
As the soft music in the background plays.
It will be a moment I cherish with my kids
When they ask me what love is.

It was extremely nerve wracking, but calm, and absolutely amazing.
That was the place I was meant to be in that exact moment.
I knew that for sure.

Leaning my head against your chest,
With your arms wrapping around me,
Holding me up.

The eye contact we made,
Was as if we were transferring messages,
Mind reading what the other was saying.

<u>I love you</u>

The way our bodies fit together and how you kissed my scars.
I never knew something could be so comforting.
Even with the complete fear I had,
You pushed those nerves away with the soft touch of your lips.

I can't get you out of my head.
Our moments. The times we cried together.
The times you held me and told me how beautiful I was.

I can't stop thinking of how I fit with you so perfectly,
You recited that we were <u>made for each other.</u>
Some universal fate I didn't believe in until meeting you.

I'm in so much pain.
My body misses your touch just as much,
If not more, than it needs oxygen to breathe.
It made everything go away.
 <u>Just make it go away</u>

I am screaming and yelling for help.
I'm crashing down.
Please just come back to me.
<u>Why won't you come back</u>

Take me away.
I've been suffering.
I can't keep putting on a facade.
I can't keep acting like I'm okay.
<u>I am exhausted</u>

I miss the warmth
Of your body against mine,
So badly.
It's a painful aching inside of me.

I miss seeing how happy you were over the small things.
The excitement that lit your face up with a wide, contagious, smile.

<u>The first time you got me flowers,</u>
<u>The first time I wrote you a love note,</u>
<u>And the first time you read me yours.</u>

I especially miss how adorably nervous you were
To give me the promise rings that fit me so well
Physically, emotionally, and in every way possibly,
<u>Just like the two of us</u>

Or so I thought.

<u>Why did you push me away</u>
<u>Why did you let me push you away</u>

<u>Your other half,</u>
Your mother would refer to me as.
It took me a while to realize
How much of that was true,
Because now I see
I'm not whole without you.

I still can't sleep in my room.
Too many memories of you everywhere,
But I can't bring myself to erase what we had.
<u>Not yet, just a little longer.</u>

The water streaming from my eyes
Is now rolling down my face.
From under my eye, down to my cheek,
Where you once wiped them.
Nurturing me, like I was the love of your life.

<u>You're</u>
<u>Still</u>
<u>Mine</u>

My heart is so heavy it feels as though someone grabbed the whole of it,
And is tugging at me from the bottom of an endless pit.

I'm trying so hard
To not let go
<u>I will keep fighting</u>

I hate that movies, and books
Give us a false view of the world.
They aren't realistic.

I wanted to fall in love
More than anything, when I was little.
Now sometimes, I wish I never did.

Why don't they tell you the pain that comes along with it?
Why don't they prepare us for the toxicity?

It was still love.
<u>Maybe not the right way to love</u>
But it was still <u>love.</u>

# 3. Lost Again

Words can't even describe the thoughts flooding my mind right now.
The memories,
All at once,
Scrambling inside my head.
<u>I can't shut it out</u>
<u>I'm losing myself</u>

When I was with you, your presence alone made clear of those thoughts.
In my mind all I needed was you.

You were like a drug,
You got me addicted.
And now I'm going through withdrawal.

Your love,
It always brought me back.
Whenever I would silently torture myself,
In my own thoughts,
You called out to me.
And I'd retrace my steps
Coming back from anywhere but the present.
<u>Coming back to life</u>

The memory of you pierces my heart,
And makes it feel as though
It's dropped into my stomach.
I would remain crying,
If all my tears weren't already dried out.

Afraid to close my eyes
Due to the burn left from the withered away tears,
I can't keep them open.
It hurts, but I'm hurting more,
Seeing you everywhere.
You are in everything.

<u>My first real anything</u>
<u>And my first real everything</u>

I taught my heart how
To specifically close itself off,
From things that might make it feel again.
I taught it to push everyone out,
Far away so it can never be touched.
And the one time I didn't follow that rule,
I was shown exactly why it was one in the first place.

I haven't showered in days,
Knowing the next time
Will be me washing off
Your touch,
Your scent,
Your words,
And your love.

As the sound of the
Trickling droplets rushing to the floor,
Fills my ears,
It washes everything away.

The joy you once filled my body,
The nights I spent sobbing alone,
Meaningless words that meant everything to me.

Unable to stand,
I fall to my feet curling up like I've created a shell.
Bringing my knees to my chest,
And holding myself like you once did,
I sit in silence as the water mixes with the tears rolling off my cheeks.
Convincing myself that letting you go is the best option.

The only option

I know I'm melting.
The water is boiling.
But I can't feel it,
Letting it merge with my body that is now liquid.
All I can think about
Are the way your fingers slung through mine
<u>Perfectly.</u>

Your hands through my hair,
Letting the soap cleanse and fall beneath us.
As we lean on each other under the warm water,
Everything is you.
<u>And I am drowning again.</u>

I never blamed you, and I still don't to this day.
But each year as I blow out the candles on my birthday,
I can't promise you I won't be wishing
We could've met another time.

Maybe when both our minds
Were more mature and less broken.
Maybe I could've really made you happy.
<u>Maybe we would have worked</u>

<u>I want someone to be in love with me,</u>
<u>To the point where I'm the shelter they need to survive.</u>
<u>I want to be someone's home.</u>

I just never told you
It would not matter
Unless it was you.

I never wanted to convince someone to care about me,
But I'd do it a million times just to have you.

<u>I don't want to be with you</u>
<u>Because I need love,</u>
<u>And I can't get that loving you.</u>

I know it's true,
I know I deserve better,
But I don't care anymore.

<u>I miss loving you</u>

I miss your laugh.
I miss your smile.
I miss your presence.
I miss you.

I miss our talks.
I miss our naps.
I miss our dreams.
What do I do?

That was,
Until it was too good to be true.

It was almost like everything,
Was a lie.

On some days it was a fairytale,
That my inner child would have dreamed of living.

On others,
I became so used to the only thing receiving for weeks,
Was a silent treatment.

In my head.
If you love someone you fight for them.
If you love someone you work it out.
<u>It all made perfect sense.</u>

So naturally my abandonment issues,
from years of trauma,
Could not take it any longer.

Dealing with a tiny miscommunication so often,
That I would constantly worry it'd be
What made you walk away,
Set my anxiety through the roof.

<u>I couldn't lose you</u>
<u>I needed you</u>
<u>I still need you</u>

I thought you knew my insecurities
Submerged my every thought and move.
I can't convince someone I'm good enough,
When I continuously fail to believe it myself.

So now the tears that once fled my eyes return.
<u>I thought I was all out of those.</u>
Suddenly, as it's blurring my vision,
I can feel a large lump
Forming in my throat.
I clench onto whatever memory
I have of you,
Silently, draining all the water my body has stored.

<u>I told you that you were worth it</u>

<u>I told you that you were worth it</u>

<u>And I wish I believed you</u>

Carefully, practicing like Van Gogh,
I painted the return of those once faded red lines.

<u>I deserve it</u>
<u>I hurt you</u>
<u>I'm sorry</u>

<u>I told you I chose my wants over my needs</u>

<u>Unfortunately that is exactly where you went wrong</u>

As someone who loves you,
How can I sit back and watch both of us hurt ourselves,
Planning a false future only with each other.

We convinced ourselves it would work,
Knowing how toxic we were.

We wanted each other so badly,
We swore we were in love.

Maybe it was just infatuation.
Toxic, toxic, infatuation.

<u>Or maybe it's just easier</u>
<u>To deal with this way</u>

<u>I can't keep putting you over</u>
<u>Everyone including myself</u>
<u>The pain hasn't stopped</u>

And I finally give up waiting for you to change.

I don't know if it's breaking you as much as it's breaking me,
But if it is, I'd be falling apart even more.
Like tiny shattered pieces,
resembling the destruction of a glass vase,
Being knocked over.
<u>I am broken and cannot be put back together.</u>

Words I previously shared with you,
Still linger in my everyday thoughts.
I pull up the screen and read what I once wrote.
<u>I miss our stupid conversations.</u>

My eyes are swelling up,
And I'm fighting the tears.
It hurts.
My mind hurts.
Everything hurts.
Part of my soul feels like it's been ripped out.
What am I without you?
<u>And who will I become</u>

Anywhere I go,
I feel out of place,
Like something is still missing.

Torn and alone, it's inevitable,
I'm falling apart.
Like a used, rundown car,
That always returns to a repair shop to get <u>fixed.</u>

My heart and mind are fighting each other
Over a boy who has hurt them both.

<u>Why didn't you fight for me?</u>
You never once did.
Not in the way my heart would die on a battlefield for you.

And it did.
Several times.

I still can't decipher whether you
Were in love with me,
Or just the way I made you feel.

I think it's easier to deal with
When accepting the latter,
<u>So that's just what I'll do</u>

I'm worried I might forget the sound of your voice.
But I'm more worried
I won't be able to fight what it does to me,
Just in case I do hear it.

<u>Please</u>
<u>Say nothing</u>
<u>But tell me</u>
<u>Just about everything</u>

Your scent remains existing in my room.
Occasionally reminding me that I can't forget you.

The silence is suffocating,
And the clutter of thoughts
Are causing migraines
To take up all the space inside my head.
It's confusing and torturing.

Similarly,
The same effect
Of the cold words,
You once spoke towards me.

<u>Empty</u>
<u>Nothing</u>
<u>Lost</u>

All the words in my head that fittingly describe what I am now.
The tears are all gone,
But so are my emotions.
Like flicking a switch,
I turned it off,
And I'm finally left
With being numb.